DISCOVER 🐾 DOGS WITH
THE AMERICAN CANINE ASSOCIATION

AMERICAN CANINE ASSOCIATION, INC.

ACA

America's Largest Veterinary
Health Tracking Canine
Registry

OFFICIAL SEAL ®

I LIKE

FRENCH BULLDOGS!

Linda Bozzo

It is the Mission of the American Canine Association (ACA) to provide registered dog owners with the educational support needed for raising, training, showing, and breeding the healthiest pets expected by responsible pet owners throughout the world. Through our activities and services, we encourage and support the dog world in order to promote best-known husbandry standards as well as to ensure that the voice and needs of our customers are quickly and properly addressed.

Our continued support, commitment, and direction are guided by our customers, including veterinary, legal, and legislative advisors. ACA aims to provide the most efficient, cooperative, and courteous service to our customers and strives to set the standard for education and problem solving for all who depend on our services.

For more information, please visit www.acacanines.com, e-mail customerservice@acadogs.com, phone 1-800-651-8332, or write to the American Canine Association at PO Box 121107, Clermont, FL 34712.

Published in 2017 by Enslow Publishing, LLC.
101 W. 23rd Street, Suite 240, New York, NY 10011

Library of Congress Cataloging-in-Publication Data
Names: Bozzo, Linda, author.
Title: I like French bulldogs! / Linda Bozzo.
Description: New York, NY : Enslow Publishing, 2017. | Series: Discover dogs with the American Canine Association | Includes bibliographical references and index. | Audience: Ages 5 and up. | Audience: Grades K to 3.
Identifiers: LCCN 2016020285| ISBN 9780766081345 (library bound) | ISBN 9780766081321 (pbk.) | ISBN 9780766081338 (6-pack)
Subjects: LCSH: French bulldog—Juvenile literature.
Classification: LCC SF429.F8 B69 2017 | DDC 636.72—dc23
LC record available at https://lccn.loc.gov/2016020285

Printed in China.

To Our Readers: We have done our best to make sure all websites in this book were active and appropriate when we went to press. However, the author and the publisher have no control over and assume no liability for the material available on those websites or on any websites they may link to. Any comments or suggestions can be sent by e-mail to customerservice@enslow.com.

Photo Credits: Cover, p. 1 Vivienstock/Shutterstock.com; p. 3 (left) Square Dog Photography/Moment/Getty Images; p. 3 (right) Istvan Csak/Shutterstock.com; p. 5 Irina Kozorog/Shutterstock.com; p. 6 Patryk Kosmider; p. 9 Creatista/Shutterstock.com; p. 10 kavalenkava volha/Shutterstock.com; p. 13 (left) Kittibowornphatnon/Shutterstock.com; p 13 (right) © iStockphoto.com/jclegg (collar), Luisa Leal Photography/Shutterstock.com (bed), gvictoria/Shutterstock.com (brush), In-Finity/Shutterstock.com (dishes), © iStockphoto.com/Lisa Thornberg (leash, toys); p. 14 © iStockphto.com/JMichl; p. 15 Tannis Toohey/Toronto Star/Getty Images; p. 17 Patryk Kosmider/Shutterstock.com; p. 18 Ariel Skelley/The Image Bank/Getty Images; p. 19 photo by Christopher Hall/Moment/Getty Images; p. 21 Veda Wildfire/Shutterstock.com; p. 22 Rawpixel.com/Shutterstock.com.

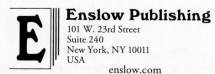

Enslow Publishing
101 W. 23rd Street
Suite 240
New York, NY 10011
USA
enslow.com

CONTENTS

IS A FRENCH BULLDOG RIGHT FOR YOU?

French bulldogs make great family pets. If you live in an apartment, a French bulldog may be a good choice for you. These dogs are not very active. They do not need a lot of space.

French bulldogs, sometimes called Frenchies, are famous for their adorable "bat" ears.

A DOG OR A PUPPY?

French bulldogs can be easy to train as long as you make it fun. If you do not have time to train a puppy, an older French bulldog may be better for your family.

French bulldogs will grow to be small to medium in size.

French bulldogs are fun-loving pets.

LOVING YOUR FRENCH BULLDOG

With big round eyes, it will be hard not to love a French bulldog. Show him love by scratching his belly!

EXERCISE

French bulldogs need only short walks on a **leash**. They do not need a lot of exercise. They will enjoy playing games like **fetch**.

Exercise should be limited in warm weather. French bulldogs can overheat.

FEEDING YOUR FRENCH BULLDOG

French bulldogs enjoy their food, so their diet must be watched.

Dogs can be fed wet or dry dog food. Ask a **veterinarian** (vet), a doctor for animals, which food is best for your dog and how much to feed her.

Give your French bulldog fresh, clean water every day.

Remember to keep your dog's food and water dishes clean. Dirty dishes can make a dog sick.

Do not feed your dog people food. It can make her sick.

Your new dog will need:

a collar with a tag

a bed

a brush

food and water dishes

a leash

toys

GROOMING

French bulldogs **shed**. This means their hair falls out. Your French bulldog will need to be brushed every day. Wrinkles around his face need to be cleaned and kept dry.

Use a gentle soap made just for dogs.

Your dog will need a bath every so often. A French bulldog's nails need to be clipped. A vet or **groomer** can show you how. Your dog's ears should be cleaned, and his teeth should be brushed by an adult.

WHAT YOU SHOULD KNOW ABOUT FRENCH BULLDOGS

Due to their short noses, French bulldogs can have breathing problems.

French bulldogs should never be left alone around water. They are poor swimmers.

Some French bulldogs will wheeze and snore.

French bulldogs do not handle very hot or very cold weather well.

French bulldogs
rarely bark.

You will need to take your new dog to the vet for a checkup. He will need shots, called **vaccinations**, and yearly checkups to keep him healthy. If you think your dog may be sick or hurt, call your vet.

A GOOD FRIEND

French bulldogs can live as long as twelve years. That is a lot of time to enjoy this dog, who will keep you smiling. French bulldogs will steal your heart by acting silly or by napping on your lap.

NOTE TO PARENTS

It is important to consider having your dog spayed or neutered when the dog is young. Spaying and neutering are operations that prevent unwanted puppies and can help improve the overall health of your dog.

It is also a good idea to microchip your dog, in case he or she gets lost. A vet will implant a microchip under the skin containing an identification number that can be scanned at a vet's office or animal shelter. The microchip registry is contacted and the company uses the ID number to look up your information from a database.

Some towns require licenses for dogs, so be sure to check with your town clerk.

For more information, speak with a vet.

There are many dogs, young and old, waiting to be adopted from animal shelters and rescue groups.

fetch To go after a toy and bring it back.

groomer A person who bathes and brushes dogs.

leash A chain or strap that attaches to the dog's collar.

shed When dog hair falls out so new hair can grow.

vaccinations Shots that dogs need to stay healthy.

veterinarian (vet) A doctor for animals.

Read About Dogs

Books

Britton, Tamara L. *French Bulldogs.* Minneapolis, MN: Abdo Publishing, 2013.

Schuh, Mari C. *French Bulldogs.* Minneapolis, MN: Bellwether Media, 2016.

Websites

American Canine Association Inc., Kids Corner
acakids.com
Visit the official website of the American Canine Association.

National Geographic for Kids, Pet Central
kids.nationalgeographic.com/explore/pet-central/
Learn more about dogs and other pets at the official site of the National Geographic Society for Kids.

INDEX

31192021628712